NIC PERverseRY

with Illustrations by Laura Coppolaro

Nick Perry

x

WATER CURTAIN CAVE

To Laura Coppolaro, whose fabulous, jolly and gentle illustrations are an absolute joy to behold

To my old sparring partner Charlie Ottley – a great source of inspiration and an endless fount of wit, wisdom and wickedness

To Mark, Andrew, Michael and Sarah for their unwavering support and encouragement

To Paula Prince, my mentor, and to Bill Coles for laying the foundations

Copyright: Nicholas Perry MMXII

for additional copies contact:
Water Curtain Cave Press
34 Crooms Hill
London
SE10 8ER
publisher@watercurtaincave.com

I dedicate this book to my parents

THE AUTHOR AND THE ILLUSTRATOR

Nick Perry has been playing with words since he first learnt to speak. This collection of verse is largely inspired by his love of twisting old jokes to slyly poke fun at his friends. Friends retort that a twisted old joke is precisely what he is!

'Nick Perry's PERverseRY' considers the foibles of our fellow men and women and the craftiness of our feathered and four-legged friends.

Laura Coppolaro is a freelance illustrator and cartoonist. She lives and works in St Ives, Cambridge.

CONTENTS

COUNTRY TALES–ROSE COTTAGE

As Plumridge drove into the village
He gave a heartfelt groan,
He'd left his satnav in his other car
And also his mobile phone;
He was heading to see an old school pal
Who'd moved to a country retreat,
He drove around to find the house
Where they'd agreed to meet.

He saw a village local
And he stopped to ask the way,
'Good afternoon,' said Plumridge,
'And how are we today?'
This unctuous introduction
Was met with veiled contempt,
As on the wooden five-bar gate
The village local leant.

'I wonder if you can help me?
I'm looking for Rose Cottage,' he said.
The rustic screwed his eyes tight shut
And shook his ancient head,
'Rose cottage? Said the countryman,
Tipping his old felt hat,
'Rose cottage in this village?
'I can't say's I've heard of that.'

Plumridge sighed and spoke again,
Shuffling his well-shod feet,
'Rose Cottage is in this village,
I believe it's in Church Street.'
'Church Street?' said the villager,
Wiping the brim of his hat,
'Church Street you say, in this village?
'No, I've never heard of that.'

With exasperation Plumridge growled
At the thought of his fruitless search,
'Church Street is in this village,
'Perhaps it's the one with the church?'
'Church you say?' said the countryman,
Tipping back his hat,
'Church you say in this village?
'No, I've never heard of that.'

'This village idiot' thought Plumridge,
Deserves a kick in the crotch,
Suppressing the desire to do so,
He said, 'well you don't know much.'
The countryman thought for a little while
Before he gave his reply,
'You're right I suppose, I don't know much,
But I'm not lost am I?'

Country Tales–The Village Inn

The evening in the village inn
Was filled with convivial charm,
(Though the amount the village folk there drank
Might fill you with alarm.)
Here Plumridge stood at the old oak bar
And offered a local a drink,
The offer was taken the drink poured and drunk
Before he'd time to think.

'You're thirsty,' observed our friend Plumridge
And he promptly offered another,
The village local accepted the drink
And suppressing a giggle said, 'Brother,
'I suppose you think you're generous,
'Buying me all these beers.'
'Not really,' came Plumridge's insouciant air
'Fancy another one?' 'Cheers!'

'There's a fellow in this village
'Who's a lot more generous than you,
'I tell you about his generous ways
'And every one of them true,
'He'll buy you drinks all night at the bar
'And take you out for a meal,
'Then back to his in his fancy car
'An E-type with wire wheels.

'He'll give you the finest brandy,
'You can sleep in his four-poster bed,
'The chauffeur will take you back home in the Rolls,
'It's true, every word I've said.'
'Good grief!' replied Plumridge astoundedly
At the tale of this generous mister,
'Has he done this for you then, my new-found friend?'
'No, but he has for my sister!'

Country Tales–The Walk

A walk across the meadows
Is one of those country delights
That easily beats the city's streets
And easily betters its sights;
Here Plumridge went for a stroll next day,
He promised to be back by tea
He walked for hours, admiring the flowers
Then sat by an old oak tree.

Not realising the time that had passed him by
(He'd promptly fallen asleep),
He stood up and strolled to a shepherd
Who was nearby tending his sheep.
'Excuse me sir,' said Plumridge,
In his usual imperious tone,
'I wonder do you have the time, old chap?
'I'm lost without my phone.'

The village local thought for a bit
As he sat by his sheep on the floor,
Then lifting the standing sheep's dugs with one hand,
He declared 'It's half past four.'
'My word,' said Plumridge,, amazed at the skill
Of this yokel in his rustic hat,
'From the feel of the teat, you can tell the time?
'However do you manage that?'

The countryman laughed and laughed and laughed,
'Til the hillside itself seemed to rock,
Then he answered with wit, 'When I lift this sheep's tit,
'I can see the village clock.'

Ben and Betty

Ben and Betty were off to get married;
They decided not to in church,
But plumped for the registry office
And waited three weeks for the search.

All was declared to be legal,
Above board, and nothing to worry,
So they both invited their families
And rushed to hitch up in a hurry.

'I'm Ben' and 'I'm Betty,' they said to the clerk,
In a breathless excitable haste;
'Hold your horses one moment,' he answered the pair,
As he studied them both, ashen-faced.

'Ben? You say Ben? Is that your full name?
' I'm not sure I can write Ben in't book;
'You'll have to go up to the births department
'And ask the clerk there to look.'

Well, Ben wasn't pleased at this slowing of pace,
But they went off upstairs in a hurry;
They came back in a race with a smile on Ben's face;
He said, 'Benjamin Braddock from Surrey.'

'Benjamin Braddock,' wrote the clerk in longhand,
Occasionally licking his pen,
'Now, Betty can't be your proper name love
'You'll have to go upstairs again.'

As the clerk turned the page they were seething with rage,
But went off with nary a word,
They came back in a while both wearing a smile,
She said, 'Elizabeth Amelia Bird.'

The clerk took his pen and wrote down her name,
He told them, 'You're lucky I'm here,
'Without full listed names it isn't the same,
You wouldn't be married my dear.'

'Neither you nor he would be legal you see,
'Your children technical bastards that's true!'
'That's funny,' said Ben as he picked up the pen,
'That's what man upstairs said about you!'

Father Patrick Fergus O'Toole

Father Patrick Fergus O'Toole
Had one simple golden rule:
To find the answer without a doubt
 Say nothing and the truth will out;
He'd heard it all, each man's obsession
Each time that he took confession.
Sins are many and each one varies,
Punished with a few Hail Marys,
He'd ask the sinner to be humble and meek,
But knew he'd be back the following week.

His own life was free of behaviour lubricious,
His sin, if it were one, was being suspicious,
Listening to all in his neighbourhood,
Not trusting the men to be kind and good,
And considering all women with an attitude chary,
Not one of them could be as saintly as Mary.
He decried misbehaviour and determined his priests
Were saintly as he, not behaving like beasts.

One afternoon he decided to call
On a junior priest who lived by St Paul's;
Young Father O'Connor opened the door,
Behind him the housekeeper was sweeping the floor,
She looked up and smiled at old father Pat,
As he entered the house and took off his hat,
'Will you no have some tea father?'
            said the pretty young maid,
Come straight to the parlour, the table is laid.'

The two men said a prayer and ate a high tea,
 And agreed all the things that two priests will agree:
The sermons they'd preach and the blessings they'd give
To teach the parishioners how they should live.
Throughout the proceedings Father Pat didn't pry,
But noticed O'Connor catch the housekeeper's eye.
Convinced in his mind that they both had transgressed,
He did what he thought would answer his quest,

He picked up the cake slice when neither was looking,
(O'Connor was eating, the housekeeper cooking)
Put it into his pocket and finished his food;
'Thanks for the meal; I don't want to be rude,
I'll just pop upstairs to pay nature a call'
So saying, he went up the stairs in the hall.
Returning, he thanked them and smiled to himself
As he picked up his bible that lay on the shelf,
'I've a number of visits to make later on
'So I bid you good evening, I'd better be gone.'

The following week Father Seamus O'Connor,
Whilst opening the sideboard on which stood the Madonna,
Noticed the cake knife was missing, 'My God!
Father Pat must have nicked it, the sinful old sod!'
'Don't accuse him of anything!' the housekeeper said,
'Why don't you send him a letter instead?
'Write you're not saying he took it
          and you're not saying he did not,
'But it's been missing since last he sat here at this spot!'

A day or two later there came a reply:
O'Connor said, 'Read it aloud or shall I?'
The letter was opened and here's what he wrote:
'Dear Father O'Connor, I don't look for the mote
'I'm not saying you're sleeping
      with your young housekeeper
'And I'm not saying you're not,
      but this lesson I'll teach you,
'You've not slept in your own bed, and this much I vow:
'If you had, you'd have found that cake slice by now!'

LORD ARTHUR MULLIN'S LAST BEQUEST

When Arthur Mullins lay down to die,
It was with a most reluctant sigh,
Throughout his life he had acquired
More wealth than most: he had retired
And thought to spend his latter years
Spending all his cash on beers,
Fine wines and women, so he thought,
And marvelled at all the things he'd bought:
A Ferrari, Rolls and Maserati,
A peerage from the Labour Party,
A lovely house in the south of France,
A Jackson Pollock – worth a glance -
Which hung in pride in his chateau
And gave his heart a rich warm glow

Was one of many of his delights
That comforted him on winter nights;
But all in vain; his doctor said
That very soon he would be dead.

So summoning up his final strength,
He decided he would speak at length
To his lawyer, doctor, priest;
These are the words of the now deceased:
'I've had a good life as you know,
'But now friends, it's my time to go,
'So this is my will and testament.'
So said he and on he went,
Listing those who'd earned a merit:
Family members who'd inherit,
Giving some to charity,
And lastly turning to the three
Who stood before him, he averred,
'Some many years ago I heard
'About an old Egyptian man
'Who, at the end of his life's span,
'Asked each mourner at his wake
'To pay a tribute for pity's sake:
'A gift of wine or simple token,
'So when the dead are reawoken
'They've a gift for the ferryman
'Who takes them to the Promised Land.
'Will you do this thing for me?'
He uttered to the standing three.

They all agreed and went away,
Returning on the funeral day.
Lord Mullins had a handsome stash:
Three hundred grand of it in cash
Was placed into three envelopes,
And handed to the self-same blokes
Who'd listened to his last bequest:
'This goes in to the coffin chest'
The envelopes in three small baskets
Were placed inside Lord Arthur's casket
Without reluctance or consternation
Before the assembled congregation
At Lord Mullins' funeral feast
By the lawyer, doctor, priest.

Later in the limousine
The clergyman's face turned puce then green
Then white, then pink and finally red
At last he spoke, here's what he said:
'I hope you'll think it for the best,
'I've got to get this off my chest,
'I couldn't say it before the people
'But I kept twenty thou' to repair the steeple.
Did I do wrong?' The doctor said, 'No, not a bit;
'I too have kept a lot of it
'I hope I won't fall in your esteem
'But I spent fifty thou' on a new machine
'Kidney, dialysis – you know the sort?
'Do you think it wrong? Did we sell him short?'

'Oh yes indeed, indeed I do,
'And really I'm surprised at you,
'You both made a promise which you failed to keep
'To our friend who's in his final sleep.'
This last speech the lawyer made,
'He told me what to do and I obeyed.'
'You placed in the coffin a hundred K?'
The doctor said with some dismay.
The lawyer answered in some style,
With a gleaming eye and a wicked smile;
From his seat at the wheel he turned his neck,
'A lawyer always pays by cheque!'

THE DOCTOR'S RECEPTIONIST

This is a story some may know
that I've turned into rhyme,
It's about a place where people sit
till their appointment time;
They sniff and sneeze and cough and wheeze
 until they hear their name,
Then making no eye-contact,
they do the walk of shame.

We none of us will gladly say
that we have something wrong
Until we're with the doctor;
not with the waiting throng.
Receptionists in olden times
(though some say they still do)
Will ask, in front of everyone,
so, what is wrong with you?

Perhaps this is familiar to some of you out there?
All eyes pricking in your back from every patient's chair.
This then is the tale of one who experienced such a query,
As he approached reception, he was asked, 'Hello dearie,'
(At sixty-five he was not pleased to be spoken to in this way
But let it pass, he told himself, be that as it may).

She then went on to further wrong and she wouldn't let it lie;
'What are you seeing the doctor for?' She asked the patient guy.
His answer was as vulgar as it was angry and most quick,
'I'm here to see the doctor – I've a problem with my dick!'

The receptionist was as very cross as she was vain and fat
'In a crowded doctor's waiting room, you really can't say that!'
'Why not?' he answered, 'you asked me, and I replied to you . . .'
'You've embarrassed all these patients now, it really will not do.

'You should have said there was something wrong with your ear or stuff like that,
'And waited till you were with the doctor; not acting like a prat.'
'Well you shouldn't ask such questions to one whom you've just met
'If you find it so embarrassing – the answer that you get.'

He left the doctor's waiting room to calm himself outside,
But he had to see the doctor, no, he would not be denied.
He waited for a little while then came in once again,
The receptionist smiled smugly with thinly-veiled disdain.

'Yes?' she asked him sweetly, 'can I help you dear?'
His reply was what she wanted, 'It's about my ear,'
Scenting victory she smirked, he'd taken her advice,
(When the patients do as they are bid it made her job so nice);
And so she followed with another prompt, 'What's wrong with your ear?'
The patients laughed at his retort, 'I can't piss out of it my dear!'

22

THREE CHARITABLE CHAPS

Charity begins at home they say,
-and each of us, in our own special way,
Decides where we spend the money we give,
-and upon these gifts the poor must live.
Some give to man and some to beasts,
Some give to paupers, some to priests.

Three such priests were sitting over wine,
They chatted happily as they passed the time.
Their conversation ranged from days gone by,
To questions of the fellow in the sky;
Each from different faiths but mates,
They turned at last to their collection plates.
Said Patrick, 'I know you'll think this awful funny,
'But what do you do about the money?

'You see, I'm not a wealthy man myself,
'To run a parish, you need good health.
'So when I have the money from the plate you see,
'I put some for others; some for me.'
'I'm the same,' said Charles, a vicar,
'Last week I took five hundred nicker;
'I wasn't going to give all that away,
'I've lots of blasted bills to pay,
'C of E stipends aren't lavish as you know,
'So from the collection I took half or so.'

Then Patrick said, 'How do you decide?
'I do the same, but I can't hide,
'The feelings of guilt that I get every time,
'Until I hit upon my plan, I draw a line,
'Across the floor to make it fair,
'Then I throw the money right up in the air,
'If it lands upon the right hand side it's mine,
'The rest is God's – it works every time!'

'Ha! I draw a circle,' the vicar cried,
'What's mine is all the cash inside;
'Having thrown it, as you do, you see?'
'Sounds like we know what's what do you and me,'
Said Patrick, 'But what about you Chaim?
'You haven't sinned? I've told you mine!'

Chaim smiled and gave them both a wink,
Then raised his glass and took a drink,
'Well, as you know, God smiles on me,
'But I can't live on charity.
'So when I get home with my plate,
'I don't, as you, rely on fate;
'I say a prayer and drink some wine,
Then throw the money,' confided Chaim,
'Just like dividing goats and sheep,
'What lands is mine – the rest God keeps!'

PEE BREAK

Whenever Guy went off to school,
He dreaded being thought a fool;
To compensate for lack of wit,
He liked to mess about a bit,
His hand was often in the air,
Leaning forward from his chair,
As if he knew the answer – but,
That wasn't why his hand was up.
On being picked he'd shout with glee,
'Can I go? – I need a wee!'

The teacher sighed and shook his head;
 Guy clasped his hands, 'Please sir, I beg!
I'm bursting, honest, let me go!'
The teacher slowly answered, 'No,
Go to your place and sit down Guy,
I'll let you go there by and by,
First, you must not ignore me,
Sit down there and write your story.'

But Guy was not to be deterred -
Did he listen? Not a word!
He simply raised his hand again,
Sir, let me go please, you let Ben!'
'And if I did what's that to you?'
'Oh please sir please – I need a poo!'
'Don't be vulgar; now keep schtum,
I will not let you leave this room,
Until you have finished your task,
Do not presume to even ask!
Don't think I don't know your game:
Every lesson it's the same,
You tell me that you want to go,
Do you really? Do you? No!'
'Sir, sir, I'm not joking – this time it's true,
I really, really need the loo!'

Poor sir had heard it all before,
But not the splashing on the floor,
 Guy, embarrassed, simply ran,
And hurried to the toilet pan;
The teacher turning to the class,
Found they too were rushing past,
'I know that Guy can be obscene,
But what you did was really mean!'
'He can't help it sir' 'You're dead!'
We're leaving, going to tell the head!'

Poor sir sat down, and couldn't speak,
He couldn't face another week,
Let alone another year or ten,
He joined the ranks of broken men,
With heavy heart and heavy sigh,
(It will not do to make kids cry)
And so he left that noble profession,
After writing his confession.

The head was pleased to read aloud
Said letter, to a jeering crowd.
The governors mooted their intent
That sir should leave, 'by mutual consent'.
Now he's relieved of job and pension,
What's he doing now? D'you mention?
Found a job? Something independent?
Oh yes, he is a lavatory attendant.

The moral of the story is at hand:
To teachers up and down the land;
Although some kids are quite a pain,
Believe them when they make it plain,
That they have an urgent need,
Follow now this simple creed:
When they ASK if they can go,
Never, ever answer NO!

THE THINGS THEY SAY

When Johnny came home from school one day,
He turned to his father and said,
'There's a small meeting tomorrow of the PTA'
'Small?' - 'Yes, just you, me and the head!'

'Sir, do you think it is right to punish people
For things they have not done?'
'No I don't think it right,
'In fact it's quite wrong,
'But why do you ask me son?'
'Well I hoped you would give me that answer sir;
'It was driving me quite berserk,
'The reason I asked you is simple:
'I haven't done any homework!'

THE AWARD WINNING ROOSTER

The rooster is a noble bird,
In appearance quite absurd,
Strutting like a popinjay,
Around the pullets he will lay,
But masculine in every sense,
This creature's prowess is immense,
Within its grasp it has the power,
To serve five females every hour.
Owning such an impressive beast,
Would be, at the very least,
A handsome way to make a stash,
By selling chicks for piles of cash,
To own a dozen one would have thought,
That nevermore would one go short.
Such was the case of Farmer Hale,
Whose fowl are the subject of this tale.

Twelve young cocks served three hundred hens,
On Hale's 'Big Chicken Farm' in the Fens,
Jack Hale was a canny man,
He formed a most ingenious plan,
When at the market last July,
He saw a sign that caught his eye:
'Bells for sale – all shapes and sizes'
'Life's full of such nice surprises.'
Thought Jack, as he bought the lot,
Then hurried home to hatch his plot.

Each dinger rang to a different pitch,
So Jack could hear which bird was which,
To every rooster he tied a bell,
When it rang like merry hell,
He knew which bird was on the nest,
Which rooster was the horniest.
The farmer's favourite rooster, Andy,
Was very fierce and very randy,

Its bell rang loudest I recall,
One day, it didn't ring at all,
Which was a shock to Farmer Jack,
Who feared to find it on its back,
But not at all the crafty chook,
Into its beak the bell had put,
So sneakily could carry on,
And mount the next hen when he'd done.

Farmer Jack was so impressed,
He entered Andy in a test
To find THE most brainy bird,
Word got round – you may have heard –
Andy won! Oh praise the Lord!
He triumphed in two well-known awards.
 The no bell prize was the first he won,
And that was cheered by everyone;
But a glow appeared in Andy's eyes,
When he also received the pullet surprise!

THE LOVELY BERKSHIRE SOW

Farmer Fred was a happy chap,
        who'd worked hard all his life,
He lived in rural splendour
        with his dog, his horse and wife.
One day he went a-travelling,
        to a market town near Slough,
To buy some hay, a barrow
        and a lovely Berkshire sow.

On his way home that evening,
        he stopped at the farm next door,
To talk to Farmer Jack his friend,
        who owned a handsome boar.
Said Fred to Jack, 'In this here barrow
        is the sow I bought today,
Can I bring her round to mate your boar?
        I've money here to pay.'

Said Jack to Fred, 'Alright, my friend
    that sounds like a good deal.'
They fixed a price; Fred toddled off
    to the creaking of the wheel.
The following day he loaded the sow
    into his new-bought barrow,
And thought of all the money he'd make
    from selling off its farrow.

The boar did what a boar does best
    and Fred said, 'What do I owe?'
Said Jack, 'I can't take money yet
    she's not pregnant for all I know!
But when you get up in the morning,
    she may be chewing the cud,
That's normal – she ain't pregnant
    but she is if she's rolling in mud.'

The very next day Fred looked at the sow,
      she was eating grass in the rain,
So he took her in the barrow to the farm next door
      and the boar did the business again.
The day after that the same old sight
      so he wheeled her round to the boar;
That whiskered, handsome heavyweight beast
      mounted her once more.

The next day dawned and the farmer's wife
      was up before her Fred,
Who called to her in the window seat
      as he lay propped up in bed;
'If she's not eating grubs but rolling in mud
      she's up the duff – she'll farrow.'
'She's not eating grubs or rolling in mud
      – she's sitting up in the barrow!'

WIDE-MOUTHED FROG

Sitting in the jungle on an old tree log,
Was a creature known as the wide-mouthed frog.
The wide-mouthed frog was a happy little beast,
As he sat and he waited for his movable feast.
Along came a spider to the old tree log,
'Hello, little creature,' said the wide-mouthed frog.
'Tell me about yourself, what do you do?'
'I'm another forest creature just like you,
'They call me a spider and I'm small in size,
'I spin spider webs and I catch and eat flies;
'But I've never seen a creature like you,
'Tell me about yourself what do you do?'

'Well, I'm a wide-mouthed frog,' the frog replied,
'And I hop through the jungle far and wide,
'I like to eat he said, his mouth stretching wider,
'And my favourite dish is the jungle spider!'
Slurp! Gulp! Out flashed the tongue!
One big swallow and the spider was gone!

The wide-mouthed frog was a happy little beast
As he sat and he waited for his next big feast.
Along came a beetle to the old tree log
'Hello little creature,' said the wide-mouthed frog
'Tell me about yourself what do you do?'
'I'm another forest creature just like you
'They call me a beetle and I'm small in size
'I like to eat leaves and the eggs of flies
'But I've never seen a creature like you
'Tell me about yourself what do you do?'

'Well, I'm a wide-mouthed frog,' the frog replied
'And I hop through the jungle far and wide
'I eat flies and spiders - I don't wish to boast
'But beetles are what I like to eat most!'
Slurp! Gulp! Out flashed the tongue!
One big swallow and the beetle was gone!

The wide-mouthed frog was a happy little beast
As he sat and he waited for his next big feast.
Along came a snake to the old tree log
'Hello funny creature,' said the wide-mouthed frog
'Tell me about yourself what do you do?
'I'm NOT a forest creature quite like you
'I'm long and I'm thin and I sleep like a log
'And my favourite food is the wide-mouthed frog!'
The frog pursed his lips and said, 'Well, I'm amazed
'You don't see many of those about these days!'

SHAKESPEARE IN LIMERICKS

Macbeth
Macbeth, though good with a knife,
Killed sleep when he took Duncan's life,
Enough was enough,
When he took on MacDuff,
Should have turned a deaf ear to his wife!

King Lear
Don't seek out praise from your daughters,
You might hear what you shouldn't oughta,
Nor read them your will,
Till you're very ill,
It'll all end in carnage and slaughter!

Hamlet
'Oh mother! What have you done?'
Said Hamlet; but Gertrude said, 'Son,
'Your father's brown bread,
'Claud's good in bed,
'I'm a widow and I'm having fun!'

Othello
Brabantio so did abhor,
Desdemona running off with the Moor,
When Iago came,
And called out his name,
He said, 'Why, she's nowt but a whore!'

But Othello was happy at first,
Till his bubble of love Iago burst,
By sowing the seed,
 Of mistrust, yes indeed,
Emilia feared for the worst.

Othello thought, 'Cassio's stuffed her!'
He told Des he no longer loved her,
He jumped on the bed,
And covered her head
With a pillow, and that's how he snuffed her!

THE DARKLING THRUSH - PART II

I leant upon a coppice gate,
When frost was spectre grey,
The farmer came and said, 'Oi mate!
No public right of way!'

SOME FAMOUS WOMEN

Lady Godiva
Lady Godiva rode a horse
Naked through the streets of course
The horse was naked too
But that I'm sure won't interest you!

Mata Hari
Mata Hari was a spy
She was employed to lie and lie
With diplomats, who gave away
Their secrets as with her they lay;
She was caught and shot for treason,
Now she lies still and that's the reason!

Amelia Earhart
Amelia Earhart flew a plane,
And was never seen or heard again.

Dame Nelly Melba
Dame Nelly Melba liked to sing ,
Her voice, they say, was just the thing;
She liked ice-cream for which she's famed,
A dish from which a dish is named.
And thin cooked bread – another boast
Alas, the toast of toast is toast!

Indira Gandhi and Benazir Bhutto
Indira Gandhi and Benazir Bhutto
Their early deaths just go to show
That certain types of men can't stand
A woman with the upper hand.

44

THE TEST OF THREE

Keep this philosophy in mind the next time you hear,
or are about to repeat a rumour.

In ancient Greece there lived a fellow
who was as wise as he was mellow,
He avoided childish prattle
and wasn't one to tittle-tattle,
He stayed serene while others, stricken,
would react like headless chicken
To gossip, and the common weal
of slanderous hypocritic zeal.

Socrates, (for this was he)
lived in quiet serenity,
Contemplating life's great themes
— the meaning of our nightly dreams,
Moral issues of the day;
(navel-gazing some might say);
His classes taught, his family home;
he sat, content and thought alone,
When, on this sunny afternoon,
a fellow rushed into the room.
The man, a fan, fell to his knees
and shouted, 'Mighty Socrates,
I hang upon your every word,
but do you know what I've just heard?
I have news of great import,
about your pupil — I report . . .'

'Wait a moment! Hold your breath!
First you must pass a little test.'
Said Socrates so solemnly
'. . and this is called the Test of Three.'
'The Test of Three?' The young man said,
the old man sadly shook his head,
That's right before you tell me news
I must affirm your hidden views,
You are young and in one's youth
one seldom seeks to find the truth,
Before you speak let's verify
that what you say is not a lie.

46

The Test of Truth is first so do,
assure me what you say is true.'
'I can't be certain what's occurred;
in fact it's something I just heard.'
'So though this news is something hot,
you don't know if it's true or not?

Let us try the second test
— are your intentions of the best?
The Test of Goodness will tell me
if what you say is good you see?
Or if, indeed as I suppose
your news is bad . . .' the young man rose,
Impatiently he blurted out,
'No, it's not good, without a doubt . . .'
'So, you want to tell me something bad
about my student; that is sad,
Especially when you've said that you,
can't verify that it is true.'
The young man shrugged and turned quite red,
embarrassed at the things he'd said.

'Never mind, said Socrates,
we can ignore the pair of these
If you pass the final test
— it's called the Test of Usefulness.

To pass this test you must agree
that what you want to say to me
Is something useful — this I vow
—that if it is I'll hear it now.
Alas! The poor lad shook his head,
'not really' were the words he said.
'So what you want to say to me
is neither true nor good nor use d'you see?'

The young man looked down at the floor
and as to words he said no more.
Socrates smiled a smile serene
— that's why he's held in high esteem.
It also explains why in his whole life,
he didn't know Plato was shagging his wife!

THE HUSBAND STORE

For many, many women marriage is just alright,
A cheerful institution of mutual delight;
The man is a comfort and her joy
      –he dotes upon his wife,
As they go in love together
      through the journey of a life.

But for many, many others marriage is a cage.
Wives sense a loss of freedom
      and it puts them in a rage;
They want to do all they did before
      –they won't be reconciled
With staying in each night with 'him'
      and maybe a small child.

So when their days of escapades
      are very nearly through,
They try to find a matching mind
      who's honest, loyal, true;
With perhaps secure employment
      and is handsome what is more,
Such ladies go and join the queue
      outside The Husband Store.

The Husband Store is a curious place
      –women go to find a man,
Its products are there for all to see
      and labelled on the plan;
However there are simple rules
      for all who go to shop,
You may visit each floor only once
      and it's six floors to the top.

You may shop at The Husband Store but one time
      to see each of its sights,
The value of the goods augments
      as you ascend its heights;
The shopper may choose any item
      from any particular floor,
But once you're up you can't go down
      except to the exit door.

A woman arrives at The Husband Store
      to read the ground floor sign,
It says, 'These men are nice and kind,
      they'll say 'will you be mine!''
'That's cool,' she thinks, 'but I'll go up
      and check out the next floor'
So up she goes to read the sign
      upon the first floor door.

These men have jobs and are nice and kind,
      it reads but she wants more
So once again she climbs the stairs
      to reach the second floor.
These men have jobs, love kids'
      it says but she says 'No!'
So once again she mounts the stairs,
      to the third floor would she go.

These men have jobs, love kids are kind
      and also they're good-looking,
Thinks she, 'sounds good but what's above?
      Perhaps they do the cooking?'
The fourth floor sign said all the above
      plus 'these men love to cook,'
'Fantastic! But what's on the floor above?
      It's worth a little look!'

She walked on up another floor
        to read the sign which said:
'These men are like the floor below
        but also good in bed.'
She was so sorely tempted
        to go in there and then,
But the thought of just a little more
        made her mount the stairs again.

The final floor was different
        –the sign was large and bold,
The wording of it quit a shock
        –it made her blood run cold;
There are no men on this floor; it said,
        above is just the roof,
Women are impossible to please
        this floor's the final proof.'

The owner of the husband store
        thought he'd try his luck again,
Across the street he opened
        a Wives Store just for men;
The rules were the same and the men rushed in
        to see what they could find,
The ground floor women were happy,
        they were sweet and they were kind.

The women on the first floor were pretty
        They loved sex and they were funny,
The second floor women liked football too
        –and beer–and they had money;
There were four other floors in the building
        –or so it has been said,
Despite the attractions that may be there
        no man has visited!

The moral of this story if I am to be believed,
Women are perfectionists and men too easily pleased!

THE CRACKLY LINE

Whilst sitting alone in the office,
On a whim Bob picked up the phone,
He tapped in the number to call his wife
He knew she would be at home.
'Hello?' a little girl's voice replied,
 'Hello? Is that you Maddy?
'Is your mother there? Is she near the phone?
'Tell her it's your daddy.'

The line was crackly but the girl replied,
'Mummy's upstairs right now,
'She's gone to the bedroom with Uncle Pete
I think they're having a row.'

'But you don't have an Uncle Pete, my love,'
Said Bob with dawning alarm,
'I do, I can hear them shouting!'
'Alright love, just stay calm.'

'Here's what I want you to do then,
'Be quiet as a mouse,
'Go to the bedroom door then shout:
''Daddy's come back to the house!
''He's got a gun and he's angry;
''he's coming upstairs right now,
''He says he'll kill you Uncle Pete,
''And he's calling you, Mummy, a cow!''

A few minutes passed for poor, worried Bob
Before she came back on the line,
'I did what you said but now they're both dead,
'It's been a terrible time!

'They must've rushed for the window
'And jumped in the swimming pool,
'They forgot you took the water out last week,
'When I was away at school.'

A silence fell on the crackly line,
Till Bob could take it no more,
'Swimming pool did you say my love?
'Is that 27394?'

THE PILOT

To fly a plane is quite a feat
        and a significant responsibility,
A pilot must be sober, calm
        and act with deft agility;
He must always speak politely
        to the passengers, be demure,
Even when there is a problem;
        he should seek to reassure.
Bur when the plane is safely landed
        and everyone's disembarked,
He can rest, relax or have a drink
        once his vehicle is parked.

So pilots often can be found
        de-stressing in the bar,
Or joking with a stewardess
        and pushing it too far:
Away from home young hearts may roam
        — temptations always there,
When it comes to sex and drinking
        — it's much more fun to share!

One pilot, on a long-haul flight,
      let's call our hero Billy,
Had his eye on Sharon the stewardess
      — 'a pretty little filly'
(Such were the words he used at least,
      when talking to his Co)
Our story starts on landing
      as the plane began to slow.

'Thank you for flying with us today;
      we hope you've enjoyed your flight,
Look forward to seeing you soon on 'Derry Air';
      thank you and goodnight!'

Billy turned to his co-pilot, Darren;
　　　　he gave him a wicked grin,
'When I get off the plane,' he said,
　　　　'I'm getting a cool one in!
'Then maybe another but after that
　　　　— keep this quiet Darren
'I'm going to make love to that gorgeous stewardess
　　　　— you know, the new one, Sharon?'

The poor stewardess went beetroot red
and rushed down the aisle at a pace
'The pilot has left the intercom on!'
she thought as she fell on her face.

A kindly old lady, helped her up,
 'It's alright miss' she said,
'No rush, he's having two beers first
 — before he takes you to bed!'

Tom, Dick and Harry

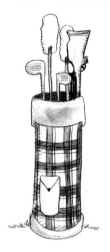

Tom, Dick and Harry were three golfing sorts,
They set off one morning for their typical sports,
A fine round of eighteen at their local club,
Then off for a drink at their usual pub.

As they approached the very first tee,
They were met by a stranger who greeted the three
And asked, 'May I join you? I play off a ten',
Being friendly and kind they agreed there and then.

Chaps being chaps they talked of their work,
Tom was a banker and Harry his clerk,
Dick told the stranger his job, 'I'm in sales',
The fourth man's reply is the start of this tale.

'I'm a hitman,' he told them as he lined up his shot,
'I could hit the church spire from this very spot.'
Dick didn't believe him till he got an eyeful
Of the golfbag in which was a powerful rifle.

The inquisitive nature of the three golfing blokes,
Was further enhanced by the gun's telescope
Attached to the barrel; said Tom, 'May I see?'
The man passed the gun to him saying, 'Feel free.'

There was no one about as Tom took the gun,
His eye at the sights and thinking, 'What fun!'
He swivelled it round to have a good look,
His heart was a-flutter his nervous hands shook,

With excitement he trembled like a very small mouse,
'Hey guys! I think I can see . . .yes! My house!'
'There's my wife in the bedroom, sitting up in bed,
'She's naked, it can't be – that's my neighbour Fred!

'He's taking his clothes off. Now he's naked as well!
'Oh God I can't take it, oh damn them to hell!'
Poor Tom passed the gun saying, 'That makes me so sick,
'I'd love to shoot that man in the . . .'

Dick, who was listening, turned to the stranger,
'Could you do it?' he asked, 'Are we within range here?'
Said the hitman 'For a fee, my usual figure
Is one thousand pounds each pull of the trigger.'

Tom couldn't wait, he said, with a sob
'That lying adulteress – shoot her in the gob,
'There's a thousand for that and another thou' more
'If you shoot off the thing that has made her his whore!'

'It's a deal' says the hitman who took up the gun
He paused, hesitated and twiddled his thumb
Then waited again as he lined up the sight,
'Come on pull the trigger, I'm nervous alright?

'What are you waiting for, please I can't stand . . .'
'Shh! Wait! I think I can save you a grand. . . !'

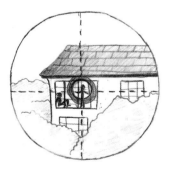

THE TALE OF MARY-JANE
(WHO DIDN'T MIND HER P'S AND Q'S)

One thing parents know is rude:
Their children's lack of gratitude.
When time and trouble have been shown,
To hear their offspring sigh and groan,
And see contemptuous eyeballs rolled,
It makes the warmest hearts grow cold.
Such was the case with Mary-Jane,
Whose parents both had tried, in vain,
To make the little madam happy,
From when she was wrapped in a nappy.

Her father, who was kind and good,
Had helped in every way he could,
He bought her toys and clothes and shoes,
And always let his daughter choose,
Whenever they went out to shop,
Mary-Jane would never stop,
She got her father to dig deep,
And buy the child a gift-wrapped heap
Of dolls and toys and games and such,
But did she answer 'thanks so much'?
Not a bit – she only said, 'Dad, drive me home'
In a most imperious tone.

The wretched father, that sad old sap,
Was not a very happy chap.
He told his wife, 'Dear, I despair,
She clearly doesn't seem to care,
She's such a selfish little pup,
It's up to you, for I give up.'
The mother, thinking she knew better,
Attempted to resolve the matter.

She took her daughter to the quack's,
And tried a hundred different tacks
To make the child appreciate
Her parents' gifts – alas! Too late!
The child, a most ungrateful chump,
Met all entreaties with a humph!
And this went on for years and years,
With nary a 'ta' or 'thanks' or 'cheers';

The money spent on boarding schools,
Trips abroad and rings and jewels,
Riding lessons, theatre trips,
Elicited nothing from her lips.
One would have thought that now she'd be
Alone, at home in misery,

But not a chance of that my readers, no,
Mary had the sense to go
And join the so-called old rat race,
To find employment at a place
Where there was never need for thanks:
She now works at a Merchant Bank's;
She's paid in millions – yes it's true
The money mostly comes from you!
Her motto: 'Leave manners on the shelf,
'When offered, always help yourself!'

CHARLES AND HIS FAVOURITE TOY

Every little girl and boy,
Has one particular favourite toy:
A teddy bear, a box of bricks,
Compendium of conjuring tricks,
A glockenspiel, computer game,
A sailing boat, electric train.
The simple pleasure each toy brings,
Can mean a million different things

To every child – and every mum,
To know her offspring's having fun;
And as the child gets to his teens,
The toy may change but not, it seems,
The happiness each one may feel,
Is not lessened nor yet less real,
But if the toy is one he had,
From since the boy was just a lad,
Well then his folks will start to question
The subject of the youth's affection.
Such was the case of Master Charles
Who, thinking hard about 'the girls',
(A Scottish accent here please note,
To sound the words the poet wrote);
Would take his favourite source of joy
And play with it – 'It's not a toy!'
His mother, watching, told him straight,
'It is Mum!' he'd ejaculate.
The fun it brought him, sad but true,
Only grew and grew and grew,
Until Charles groaned at his confession:
'My favourite toy is an obsession!'
He'd sadly grown so fond of it,
But couldn't stop – no not a bit,
His pastime playmate, sad to say,
Was toyed with every night and day;

When friends arrived to ask him out,
He'd only sulk and scowl and pout,
Then hurry off alone, he went,
Till all his pleasure source was spent.
And pretty soon he had no mates,
While other boys went out on dates.
His mother knew it had to end,
On parting from his final friend,
Who'd sniggered when she told him, 'Nick,
He won't come out he's feeling sick.'
The doctor pretty soon was called,
(A portly man and somewhat bald);

'My diagnosis' said the doctor,
'He must stop playing with his 'Chopper'!'
(Such was the name that Charles had used
For that which he had long abused);
But when his mother told him, 'Stop!'
He only got into a strop,
And carried on with renewed vigour,
To try to make his wee toy bigger.
Alas the thing had grown so worn,
(He'd played with it since he was born)
That pretty soon it worked no more.
The pleasure that Charles had in store
For ladies, he would one day find,
Was now all gone – and he was blind!
Yes, vanished now was poor Charles' sight;
He knew the reason for his plight.
Today he spends his adult life
Alone, at home, without a wife,
Bereft of friends – he'd come a cropper,
And all because his little 'Chopper'
Had led this raddled youth astray,
And left him where he is today.
So boys, be warned, a little pleasure
From that thing that all boys treasure,
Is better left in those safe hands,
Of one who really understands!

PAULA RANG

Paula rang this morning, she told me,
    'Nick, guess what?
I've booked the Cloisters venue
    for a Wednesday evening slot,
I've put you in the Festival
    with publicity – the lot!'
A Wednesday evening slot? My God!
    'Sure, fine that's really great!'
I'd better start to write some poems
    before it's all too late,
I'd better schmooze the elusive muse
    or my head is on a plate.
But what to write? I know not what
    my mind has gone a blank

If I arrive with nothing
    I'll have no one else to thank
A month to write some poems!
    - my heart, at this point, sank.
I picked up a pen and opened a book
    then made myself a drink
I looked out in the garden
    to give me time to think
I put my pen to paper
    but then ran out of ink.

71

Oh this is hopeless, dearie me!
        What will the people say?
'He's supposed to be a poet
        – we've heard nothing new today
If the next one up's as bad as this
        – that's it – I'm on my way!'
I know, I'll ring my poet pal
        bounce around some ideas
Politics, religion, sex
        - our hopes and dreams and fears
We'll plan an epic poem
        and then hit the pub for beers.

I awoke today with aching head
        I'd got into a fight
And forgotten all our brilliant plans
        I cut a sorry sight
So here I must apologise:
        I've nowt to say, goodnight!

THE TRAFFIC POLICEMAN

Never speed – it ruins lives,
Makes widows out of happy wives,
Leaves children orphans or even worse,
Let's face it, speeding is a curse.
But how we moan when asked to stop,
By the poor, benighted traffic cop.

This story tells of one such man,
He'd reach the middle of life's span,
And very near the shift's end, he
Was having thoughts of home and tea,
When, down the road there came a car,
At breakneck speed, a Jaguar.

The driver, not the usual kind,
Not a drunk out of his mind,
Nor a drug-crazed adolescent,
But Mrs O, The Larches, Cheshunt.
The copper stopped her then he asked her,
'Could you drive that any faster?
'Was this an emergency
'Tell me, why the urgency?

'Your licence please.' he next enquired.
'Sorry sergeant it's expired.
'Drink driving; that's the fourth time now!'
The copper thought. 'You stupid cow.'
But said, 'Your logbook then is it to hand?
'And by the way, you're nicked and banned.'

'No logbook either, for you see
'This car does not belong to me,
'It's owned by a man I had to shoot
'His body parts are in the boot.'
PC Bennett called back to base
A worried look upon his face.

Pretty soon the back-up came,
D.I. Simpson was his name,
Armed, but in civilian suit,
He slowly said, 'Open the boot.'
Whilst pointing at her with his gun,
She strangely seemed to find it fun.

The boot was empty! 'Be so kind,
'Your papers please?' 'I think you'll find
'All the documents are in my bag.'
There was a logbook for a Jag,
It matched the registration plate,
A licence – it was up to date!

''My Sergeant told me you were banned,
 'You stole this car. I understand,
'You killed the owner, a man who
'Is cut up in the boot.' 'Not true!
'As your eyes can see,
'And none of that was said by me.

'I can't believe that's what he said.'
She replied and shook her head.
'The lying swine! Oh, I'm so vexed
'What will the bastard think up next?
'That I was speeding I suppose?'
At this point she blew her nose.

Simpson put his gun away,
He told her to be on her way;
'But may I first apologise,
'For Sergeant Bennett's nasty lies;
'Demoted to the ranks he'll be,
'Just you leave it all to me.'

The moral for the boys in blue
And all men out there, (this is true):
Never stop a woman who
Is trying to get away from you!